FINDING MY WORDS

Aphasia Poetry

FINDING MY WORDS

APHASIA POETRY

Michael Obel-Omia

With Carolyn Obel-Omia

Visit our website at
www.StillwaterPress.com
for more information.

First Stillwater River Publications Edition.

ISBN: 978-1-955123-25-9

Library of Congress Control Number: 2021913482

1 2 3 4 5 6 7 8 9 10
Written by Michael Obel-Omia & Carolyn Obel-Omia
Published by Stillwater River Publications,
Pawtucket, RI, USA.

Publisher's Cataloging-In-Publication Data
(Prepared by The Donohue Group, Inc.)

Names: Obel-Omia, Michael, author. | Obel-Omia, Carolyn, author.
Title: Finding my words : aphasia poetry /
Michael Obel-Omia, with Carolyn Obel-Omia.
Description: First Stillwater River Publications edition. | Pawtucket, RI,
USA : Stillwater River Publications, [2021]
Identifiers: ISBN 9781955123259
Subjects: LCSH: Obel-Omia, Michael--Poetry. |
Aphasia--Patients--Poetry. | LCGFT: Autobiographical poetry.
Classification: LCC PS3615.B41 F56 2021 | DDC 811/.6--dc23

The views and opinions expressed
in this book are solely those of the author
and do not necessarily reflect the views
and opinions of the publisher.

For my mother, Rosemarie Little.
1936-2000

"Words, words, words"
— *Hamlet,* Act II, scene ii

CONTENTS

ACKNOWLEDGEMENTS

There are too many people to thank for all the countless ways I have been supported throughout my stroke recovery and in publishing this book. This book is a result of the support I have had from friends and family who have been there for me since my stroke on 21 May, 2016. My recovery and ability to put this collection together would not have been possible without your friendship and love.

I am so thankful for the ARC, the Aphasia Resource Center at Boston University, led by Jerry Kaplan and all of the group leaders for their dedication and perseverance. Thanks also to my friend Denise Lowell, a fellow stroke survivor and a tireless advocate for those of us with aphasia.

As Ralph Waldo Emerson, a fellow aphasia survivor, opined, "The glory of friendship is not the outstretched hand, not the kindly smile, nor the joy of companionship; it is the spiritual inspiration that comes to one when you discover that someone else believes in you and is willing to trust you with a friendship." I am blessed to have so many people who believe in me: John Strachan, who brought music back into my life; LaRoy Brantley, whose riotous laughter always cheers me up; Erik Diekman, steadfastly loyal; Kevin Scullen, who has always been there when I need him; Velura Perry, offering patient support; and Caty and Nat Kessler, checking up on me, always positive.

To my best friend of over 40 years, Chris McEnroe, all I can say is that I couldn't do this without you. Your friendship is a constant in my life. Chris and his wife Kathy Bliss have been there to celebrate the highs and comfort me through the lows since my stroke.

My friends from Middlebury College were all there for me, filling me with "the strength of the hills." I thank Karen Hammerness, Claire Gwatkin Jones, and Sybil McCarthy for believing in me, reaching out to me, and encouraging me to share my story. Chris and Diana Sinton brought me laughter and bagpipe music when I arrived home from Spaulding. And Alison Carrier—I marvel at her constant ability to see the best in me, every single day. Chris Summersgill—for 37 years he has been encouraging, nudging, and celebrating me.

I am grateful for the support on every front from Karin Wetherill. One memory stands out—her encouragement of my getting back on the bike, pushing and pushing, even when I fell again and again. Thank you to Denise Glickman for everything—the value of your company as we both found a path forward from brain injury is immeasurable.

All of these people have been a critical part of my support network which brought me to a place where my writing this book was possible, but I want to specifically recognize Chris Summersgill, Denise Glickman, and Alison Carrier for their work reading draft after draft, deeply considering the meaning of each poem, and helping me find ways to make my voice clearer.

Family also has held me up. Thank you to Betsy and Sandy Campbell, who have been there in a million little ways for me and Carolyn since my stroke. Sandy, my father-in-law who tragically passed away just before this book's publication, greatly loved me and was a father to me. I will miss him. My sister Heather, and her family, and my loving brothers- and sisters-in-law have all found ways to support me and keep me moving forward. Of course, there are my children, my three not-so-little-anymore birds: Jackson, Liza, and Zachary. They bring joy into my life every day.

Ultimately, my wife, Carolyn. I don't know where to begin. From the moment of my stroke, when she literally saved my life, she has been by my side. From then until now, Carolyn has been there, always helping me find my words. I simply couldn't be without her; she is my inspiration, my dedication, my life, my home. She is the Penelope to my Odysseus; thank you, I love you.

INTRODUCTION
Speak the Speech by Chris Summersgill

On Sunday morning, May 22nd, 2016, I answered an awful phone call.

"Michael had a stroke, he's at Rhode Island Hospital," my friend Diek said. I left the house desperate. Was this the last time I would see my friend Michael? Was he about to die? Strokes don't happen to people as young and full of life as Michael, right? Can he move? Can he talk?

Thirty-two years prior, on move-in day at college, Michael burst into my dorm room in a thunderstorm of words. He moved on to his next new friend a minute later, but I was stunned. College was off to a loud start. I would soon come to love the unique and unforgettable enthusiasms that make up Obel's infectious personality.

Michael Obel-Omia is a teacher by profession and habit. Words are his currency and his entertainment. By his own description, Michael is a "loud, proud black man." In today's America, being loud and proud, particularly if you are a black man, can be dangerous. It can also be complicated, particularly as you guide your three biracial children to grow into confidently aware adults who embrace the world. Complications multiply if you fit none of anyone's preconceptions. If you recite Shakespeare, Eric B. & Rakim, Red Sox batting averages, and Martin Luther King Jr.'s speeches with equal frequency and fervor, you are definitively complex. Michael's complex genuine self is how he thrives in environments as diverse as elite prep schools and neighborhood barbershops. Michael is a study in contrasts—he personifies Whitman's "Song of Myself." He contains multitudes.

This magnetic, infectious, complex, walking explosion of words is the Michael Obel-Omia I have known and loved for over 30 years. Heading into the hospital that dreadful morning, I fretted, "What of Michael will I find upstairs?"

I found my friend. Completely inert. Worse, there were no words.

By late afternoon, there had still been no discernable words from Michael. He seemed to recognize his wife Carolyn, but there was no indication he could even hear anyone else. Later, after everyone else left, I sat by his bed. The room was quiet. No buzz of visitors, no machines beeping. The torrent of nurses had subsided. In the quiet, I remembered the books I grabbed while racing out of the house. I picked up *Hamlet*. One of Michael's favorites, I thought. I began reading at the only part of the play I remembered, "To be or not to be..." By the end of the soliloquy, the rhythm of Shakespeare felt less unfamiliar. No acknowledgement from Michael, so I continued through Hamlet's descent into madness, his banishment of Ophelia to the nunnery, and to the end of the scene. The players exited the stage and I closed the play. Perhaps it was time for me to leave, too.

Then, from the quiet dusk of the room, a strong clear voice, "Speak the speech, I pray you." Michael had not moved. His eyes hadn't opened. But that was unmistakably and clearly him—loud and proud! The shock of hearing his voice subsided enough for me to gather myself. What does he mean? Does he want me to keep reading? I re-opened the play and turned to the next page—Act 3, Scene ii—and read aloud, through tears of shock and wonder and relief, Hamlet's words, "Speak the speech, I pray you."

From the depths of his battered brain, Michael had retrieved and produced the next line. I felt the literal chill of the mysterious, the divine. Michael might have been inert, but he was in there.

It would be a week before Michael could leave the hospital for rehab. Even there, he couldn't speak or move much. The prognosis was not good. The damage to his brain was extensive. He would recover physically, but only some of his speech and little of his comprehension, the doctors said, and after a handful of months—a year at best—his improvement would stall.

Today, nearly five years later, Michael continues as he has every day—working hard, inexorably defying expectations, and passionately teaching all of us who will listen.

Michael works hard with experts and formal therapy, but he does more. His daily email (literally, unfailingly—daily for nearly 5 years) of personal musings and a selection of poetry that matches his mood or the day's news is part of his ongoing therapy. His public speaking, on the radio and at church, is part of his therapy. And his own poetry—the work you now hold—is part of his therapy. This work is Michael's struggle against a cerebral straitjacket, a muffling fog that obscures outgoing signals. He works hard every day to let himself out. He hears us. He reacts as he always has but is frustratingly aware that the words that make it out are not always the words he intends. This muffler, he would teach us, is the maddening curse of aphasia.

In *Finding My Words*, Michael shares himself, works to heal himself, and teaches us. Michael teaches us with the borrowed poetry of William Shakespeare, Walt Whitman, Bob Marley, and Emily Dickinson. He gives us lessons in vocabulary. We learn about aphasia clinically and intimately through Michael's revealing portraits of life after stroke.

This selection of Michael's original poetry invites us to experience aphasia from the inside. Via "Aphasia," "Haversack," and "A Conversation," Michael intimately shares different aspects of the disorienting vortex in his head. We begin to learn about aphasia clinically through "Farrago" and "A Bumper Sticker." While you're experiencing the physical challenge presented by a simple zipper in "Gratitude," you'll be introduced to new vocabulary with "Lagniappe" and absorb some Shakespeare at the same time.

In addition to using your dictionary, you'll need to do a little more work. We learn from "In Good Company" that there are 52 offerings in this volume as a reverential nod to one of Michael's muses, another poetic stroke survivor. Learning why is your homework.

We learn about aphasia through Michael's experiences and observations, two components of his multitudes. We also learn about aphasia through revelations and recitations of the person that Michael is.

The anxious father worries about his biracial son interacting with police in "A Darker Moment." The tenderly heartbreaking moments of intimate struggle for comprehension from his children is the core of "If Only I Can Speak," and the ironically titled "It's Not You, It's Me." The peaceful pride in and sheer love of his children is rendered in "Three Little Birds."

The peace, resilience, dignity, and resolve born of religion (another important aspect of Michael) arrive in "Hello," "Compline," and amusingly in "Ash Wednesday." There is more humor and a little word play in "Ms. Malaprop" and other offerings. We're guided on Michael's quieter search for peace, clarity, and a chance for the body and mind to relax and heal through "Quietus," "Waiting," and "Present Moment."

The confusing hubbub of every day is sprinkled throughout this entire volume, while the disorienting aspect of racism is addressed only briefly in "If I Had the Chance," "In This House, I Believe," and a handful of other oblique references. We'll hear more about race and politics from Michael in the future.

"Maelstrom's" vulnerability and fear, "The Black Swan's" unrelenting work ethic, the unfair humility of aphasia—they are all here and all presented directly and optimistically. Stroke and aphasia are an indelible part of Michael, but they are only a part. "Where I'm From" begins to set out Michael's multi-layered persona but it, too, is an incomplete first two chapters of an interesting life. I've known Michael for more than 35 years, yet I've learned about and from him as I have read the words he has found.

I am humbled to have been asked to share my friend Michael with you. Here you can learn about aphasia. You can find intellectual, enlightening, amusing, frustrating, frightening, angry, tender, grateful, and poignant revelations here. Like Michael himself and Whitman before, Michael's words contain multitudes.

FINDING
MY WORDS

A Conversation

Buzzing so near,
and so far.
Speaking is all around me,
so far and nearby.
Whirling, buzzing, swooping up the noise,
and yet, nothing clears away, still surrounds me.

He's so—swirl!
He has my mind—whoosh!
He's so determined—zip, zip, zip!

What does it all mean?

Gratitude

Fumbling my right arm,
I slowly, gently try to make it right.
Sweating, I can imagine the zipper sliding up
fumbling, trembling, slowly.
I will try.

On 21 May 2016, I dreamed a dream,
only, I could not get up.
I couldn't, I just couldn't.
The dream was a reality.

I couldn't walk, I fumbled my words,
a whirl of words,
logomachy: one letter, one time.

Hamlet, graceful, but aphoristic, had words for me:
words, words, words,
a little more kin and less than kind,
Heart of hearts, ay, there's the rub, but no Hamlet.
I labored him, everyone, moil with hard,
and I was, what does one say, improving?

Now, there is still the zipper.

It is a large, fluorescent Northface, refusing to follow my lead.
Fumbling with my right arm, I have patience, patience is a virtue.

I swear and sweat, moving the small zipper, I work.
Slip goes my left arm, but I am okay.
I tug and push it, I tug and pull again:
slowly, calmly, I have my zipper.
Lightly impressing, I can do it:
Zip, zip, zip: thank you.

Now, I will tie my shoes: the rest is silence.

Quietus

It snows, so silently—and yes, sweetly,
it sifts through leaden sieves, then I wait.
Cool, no, cold, frigid, icy, bitter—cold.
Begrudgingly, I crunch my pockets, and I lug my vest,
heavy, bright, phosphorescent orange, I bundle the coat around me.
It is cold, frigid, and I wonder at how gray it is—
the gray warms me.
It is dark, and, now, it shifts away, and, silently, quietly, I am warm.

Bee Stinging

Did a bee fly by?
Did the bee fly in my mind?
Why is my tongue swollen up?
I can feel the whole tongue fill my mouth,
and I cannot breathe.

Patience, friend, don't panic;
You will get by—this too, will pass.
The swelling lessens,
and I tentatively speak my mind.

Definition

Hummmm, buzz, a whirl:

"Aphasia is an impairment of language, affecting the production..."
—or—Swish! What? excuse me? I don't understand; again,
    please, damnit!
Humming, moving, clip, clip, clip,
"...and comprehension of speech and the ability to read or write."
I have no idea, again, what?
"Aphasia is always due to injury to the brain—most commonly from a
    stroke, particularly in older individuals."
"However, it does not affect intelligence."

Oh, okay, I get it.
Try it again, slowly, kindly, gently, together,
and you can hold my hands
and be with me.

Aphasia

"Who's there?"
"Nay, answer me; stand yourself, and unfold yourself!"
Or, this: "stand yourself, and unfold?
I think I have it right: "Nay, answer me; stand and unfold yourself!"
I think.
These words from Shakespeare were clear as light before.
Now they are all around me, fumbling, bumbling, stumbling,
    tumbling, all this work.
"I'm drowning here!"
All the words feel like they pull me down, down, down,
and I'm full of mud, fills my mind, speaking, and all the mud, slush
    through my field,
mud, mud, mud: slow, slowly, dilly dallying, mud, in a muck,
    oozing my words:
"I'm drowning here, I really am!"
Okay, let's start with words: but, how will I use only the write,
    or right—is that right, or, write, or, correct—or is it Orville
    Wright, 1903?
Is it correct? I think, I don't know.
Words, words, words:
Lead, lead, wind, wind, bass, bass,
Are these the words I'm looking for?
"May I please have tomorrow?"
I asked in the hospital.
No answers, they didn't understand.
Sigh.

Sow, sow, bear, bare, censor, censure, conscious, conscience, jibe, gibe,
    hail, hale, allusion, illusion, witch, which, affect, effect
Words still do not make sense.
Maddening, because they used to be mine.
Words, words, words,
one question, many questions,
Words, words, words,
patience, listen, reboot.
Does this make sense, or cents?

Waiting

Until it's time, I wait.
I listen, silenced, waiting,
all my sinews, waiting.

Until I grow, until I feel,
When I will understand, yes,
patience, I know how it feels.

Have patience with me.

If I Had the Chance

An eponymous train, mayhap to Boston,
I sit quietly, reading my iPhone.
The train conductor seethes, glares at my ticket.

"Ticket, now!"

Proudly I present my iPhone, smiling.
It wasn't there.
No ticket.
"Hey, can you use the iPhone? Tickets, now!"

Fumbling, anxiously, I read the iPhone,
Sweating, in my vision, droplets fall.

Again: "Hey! can you hear me? Tickets now!"

Within my mind, I have aphasia,
speechless: now, I am angry with words.
I sputtered out, with spittle, ptyalin,
"Excuse me, I'm aphasia, patience, please!"

What, does he pity my aphasia, or is it I'm Black?
Shuffling, lazy, no good, dark, black face.
A kind gesture or tone—is it in you?

Good Old Dog

A soft sound, snoring, gently,
as he dreams, aspirating.
Quietly, he dreams,
as he runs the gravelly sand,
fluorescent green tennis ball,
on a dock, feeling the warmth.

Suddenly, he awakens,
and the humming sound glides by,
as he imagines a sound.

Ash Wednesday

A wonderful, beautiful morning rises.
Ash Wednesday, my mind and my heart have filled up:
"Repent, and believe in the Gospel, or the dictum,
"Remember that you are dust, and to dust you shall return."
A heavy, smudge finger, listening as a stern minister frowns the cross:
"Memento quia pulvis es et in pulverem reverteris."
Lenten, what an entertainment it is.

The Sound of Silence

If you are silenced, really silenced,
a quiet, calm, a perfect sound,
almost praying, like a peaceful sound.
Listen, silence: it is beautiful.
With forgiveness, I can imagine a sound.

Just be, just please, just peace.
Be calm, relax, listen, be quiet, and be loved.
All you can do is love, love, love.
A heart is breathing, listen,
all is right in the world.

Poem to My Heart

Flip, flop
Flip, flop
Pit, pat
Pit, pat
Freeze

Four years. Almost, free
pitter, pat, what is there?
Confused, unclear, disoriented.

"At rest, the SA, sinoatrial node causes your heart to beat about 50
to 100 times each minute. During activity or excitement, your
body needs more oxygen-rich blood; the heart rate rises to well
over 100 beats per minute"

"AV node (atrioventricular node). The AV node is a cluster of cells in
the center of the heart between the atria and ventricles, and acts like
a gate that slows the electrical signal before it enters the ventricles."

Thump, thump, thump.

"Every day, your heart beats (which means it expands and contracts)
an impressive 100,000 times. That adds up to more than 2.5 billion
heartbeats in the average lifetime."

Thump, thump, thump.

The heart works as I rest,
Quietly, listening, away,
I'm unaware,
but, it is listening.

Just listen. Thump, thump, thump
That is only my heart.

Imprisoned

A bright, beautiful woman said to me,
"what, my friend, is it like with aphasia?"
I listen with my sullenness seeping down,
thinking with anger, a rage, frustration,
and everything, yes, would regurgitate.
As I am anxious to feel, think, to taste, flow'ring out, explosives
 of fireworks,
imagining words, words, words, just braying,
as if imagining, joyous, cheerful,
laughing, a rib, a joke, a jape, a riff,
smiling and laughing, together, a grin.

Oh, but now, "Aphasia," I am silent,
fettered, shackled, yes, I, too, am locked down.
With closed, hard steel, imprisoning me sadly

But, in my heart, I, too, can try to speak, thinking, expressing words:
the readiness is all.

Three Little Birds

When it is quiet, really quiet,
I imagine my three, alert children.
The eldest—mulls, ponders, and he thinks.
The second one—effervescent, joyful.
The youngest—Yahweh is remembered.

From these moments, so fully here
I can squeeze a hug, just a moment,
and, yes, they know, from me, "I love you."

Haversack

I grip the pen, I'm ready to begin, a test:
page after page, flipping images,
a hat, leaves, a yard, a bumble bee.
Flip, flip, flip, a rake, a basket, lawn,
too easy, this is way too easy
Wait, wait a second: what the heck?
Is it, a, a, a, I don't know, a haversack?
Words missing, words below me,
draining like in a sink, draining mine ears
whirling and swirling, each and every word.
Words swell mine ears, haversack,
satchel, duffel, cumbersome, no!
Lounging, cameleopard, no, damnit!
Aphasia, David Byrne, Utopia,
"Burning down the House,"
Utopia, no place,
a haversack, oats, sack bag,

Oh wait, I get it: Hammock.
Hammock.

Frustrated, I seethe.

Greek, Utopia, no place, Aphasie, Greek, "speechless."
"That swells with silence in the tortured soul."
 Yes, not a haversack, but a hammock.

Where I'm From

BEFORE

I'm from Rosemarie, a "colored woman,"
Charles, a Ugandan, and Richard, my white stepfather, too
I'm from Albany and police officers picking up my brothers
I'm from one of three Black males in a high school class of 45
and being called an Alabama Porch Monkey in upstate New York
I'm from one of two Black males in a college class of 525 in Vermont
and being told by a professor, I look so good against the snow
I'm from a school in Pennsylvania, the only African-American faculty
    member, working for a former English teacher who told jokes
    about Negroes
as the KKK marched through town twice; I got the message.
I'm from accepting a job in Boston as Charles Stuart's body floated
    in the Mystic
I'm from surviving and persevering, smiling and learning and
    growing, remaining optimistic, and believing in humanity
I'm from Roxbury Latin, one of the first two African American males
    on the faculty in its 375 history, but incredibly loved, nurtured,
    and supported
I'm from a mixed marriage with an intensely beautiful and loving wife
And I'm from Cleveland, Ohio, the first Black upper school head and
    being reminded of my race after forgetting it
I'm from fatherhood of three gorgeous, biracial children,
along for our journey and teaching me
I'm from a Quaker school and acceptance
I'm now from Providence, literally and figuratively, and intense
    multiculturalism, welcoming and warmth

I'm from Shakespeare, The Red Sox, Fenway, traveling to ballparks
    and national parks, cycling for causes, laughter, singing in the
    choirs and being inspired by good preaching; bowties,
and summers on Martha's Vineyard
I'm from complexity and am a palimpsest, a puzzle, a mosaic,
    a mirror,
A joyful, passionate connector and friend,
A lover of life, and appreciator of its journey and my path.

AFTER

I am from stroke survival,
Saturday, 21 May 2016,
I am from strength, Jackson, with his hand tightly squeezed by mine
    before surgery
I will be all right.
I am from 37 days of Spaulding Rehabilitation,
With the nurses, mostly kind, but Lindor, UGH, a cold, wet, bath.
I am from listening,
and I am slowly coming around.
I am from Velura, Teresa, Alison, Chris, John, Betsy, and always Carolyn,
Contraband barbecue and ribs.
I am from many people who love me and hug me,
I am from therapy- physical, occupational, speech.
Support group rooms where we drink bottled water and share
    our stories

I am from struggling and struggling and struggling,
I cannot be determined enough.
I am from the job of living.
I am from aphasia, from my few words uttered.
I put together my words, haltingly, caring, kindly, lovingly.
I am from silence, listening.
I am from protests and rallies and Black Lives Matter, making my
    voice heard—
Black Lives Matter!
I'm from complexity and I am a palimpsest, a puzzle, a mosaic,
    a mirror,
A joyful, passionate connector and friend,
A lover of life, and appreciator of its journey and my path.

One Pain

I ache
I burn
and it envelops me.
And I feel exhausted.
My foot hurts,
my back pains me,
each day hurts
and it all feels tight.
Seizure comes,
gasping for air,
and I am beating with my heart,
hard, fast, too fast.
This pain is too severe,
doctors ask, everyone asks,
"Where does it hurt?"
"Does it hurt when I do this?"
I can't say, I can't make them understand,
jumbling, bumbling words can't explain—

Aphasia.

But when spring enters, and the summer follows,
the easier feeling flows
Improving, every day, each day, improving.

It's Not You, It's Me

It's not me, it's you
Frustrated, fumbling—
What's its name?
The drawer, the cabinet, the kitchen—
It will not close
God, what is its name? damnit!

I glare, angrily, to try to release
In an easy, fluent way:
"Good son, could you open the cabinet,
yes, yes, look down
would you kindly separate the cabinet
and rearrange the mess of drawers?
It will take a few minutes, but could you take the pans,
    pots from the cabinet?
Thank you very much!
Except he cannot understand,
Aphasia, speechless,
I cannot talk.
I glare, I'm angry, spitting out the words, damnit!

Son, it's not you, it's me

I'm sorry:
"Speak the speech, I pray you: what do you want to say?"
I open my mouth, I speak, speak nothing—
Nothing will come of nothing, speak again—
And I am lost to this child, this son, my heart.
Nothing will become nothing.
Speak again.
 I walk away, frustrated.
Vexed, crippled.
Quietly, he walks away, leaving me
Will my child, my son, one day understand me?

Morning Light

In one beautiful light, a morning light,
I had the singular moment, a particular moment.
An unexpected light—
flip, flip, flip, iridescent, cerulean,
flip, flip, flip, azure, cobalt, indigo,
luminescence, incandescent.
Ah, winsome, a smile.
Ethereal, sapphire, cyan,
I imagine words flowing, words as lovely as lapis lazuli.
I am content.

On such a day, I can imagine sailing the ship into the gorgeous horizon,
steering the vessel.
I am the captain, and I love it.

For that moment, I felt that I knew what an unbroken morning is.

Black Pear

At the small, intimate restaurant, we meet for lunch
skipping, gliding, passing words to each other,
as a hockey puck, slips, glides, pushes,
Whoosh, goal!

The three women speaking in clips and snips of words,
talking, all chatting, all three, laughing, talking:
coronavirus, soaking in a stream of consciousness,
carnival cruise, graduation, pulmonologists, Utah,
    collectively, democratically,
the markets, skipping, will she graduate? I hope so.

As tennis becomes the game: whoosh, the fuzzy green ball
    tacks the white line,
whack, across the net—oh, backhand!

Sliding, gliding, whooshing, and whacking, one another with them,
    speaking, talking, pushing, game, set, match!
The ball, the puck, they trip me.
I can only listen, not speaking.

Check, please!

I love it, but, boy, aphasia, it swirls me up.

A Flu

All of a sudden,
a wave is crashing down, waves and waves.

Almost a trickle, slightly misting,
I feel the rain lightly.
And, then, suddenly, WOW, it hits
and it hurts: numb, gashing windows on a storm,
"Get my boats, ahoy, sound out, ahoy, reign in the storm,
     bestir, bestir!"

There is no relenting, I suffer through a hurricane, level 5.
I cannot do this, help me.

But, as the storm subsides,
I have that clear, quiet, eye of the storm, and, maybe, it will rest.

Again
all of a sudden, it hits.
A wave is crashing down, waves and waves.
And it hurts: numb, gashing windows on a storm:
"Do you not hear him? You mar our labor. Keep your cabins.
You do assist the storm."

But, as the storm subsides,
Clear and quiet will return, and maybe, I will rest.

Lazarus

I wonder, if when I had a stroke, a real stroke,
I wonder, lying on the floor, panting.
And I wonder, if I could lift my head
to reach, barely, my impotent swirling,
and if I could have reached something, something so sweet.
Lazarus died, but he rose again, rising.
I wonder, what if I lived, not a stroke,
with a stem cell, reborn, infused in me,
and a new living, alive, waking me,
now, yes, I can feel my sinewy arms,
strengthening stem cells, injecting needle,
Ah, yes, like a Colossus, akimbo,
with a stern mien, stretching, like Argus, to see a new vista,
    loving all seas.
But, I still simply suffer, like Lazarus,
reaching, feebly, to feel my hands, feckless,
and I wonder about stem cells growing,
I wonder, when will I stand, confidently?

Thank you

Lentils, peas, carrots, celery,
onions, garlic, almost sausage—
and it's soup, gathered together.
Warm, lovingly prepared in a stew,
a friend, gentle, and a kind heart,
yummy, delicious farrago.

Thank you.

A Darker Moment

At night, my son walks home thinking,
hands wrapped up, pondering, well, everything.
This is a routine, a usual walk, contemplating, thinking,
20 years old, I can imagine him at 10 years old, 12 years old.
13 years ago, around and around, wonderfully playing, fantasies,
    heroic, imaginative,
my son, playful, creating a new, fashioned world.

A whirl of light and a policeman:
"Hey, what are you doing?"
"Walking, I live right there."
"What is your license number?"

He is suspicious, this policeman. Careful; what has he done?
"I haven't memorized it. It's right here."
"Really? Are you drunk? Are you high?"
"No, officer, I live right here."

Streetlights bathe him, but no one sees.
"Let me see your license. Are you drunk? I don't like your attitude."
"I'm right here, I live here, this is my home."

"Everyone can be stopped."
"There have been many break-ins."
"We don't have racial profiling here,"
the officer tells my wife,
Officious, intimidating
The very white officer with the green eyes.

But, in a summer, light, playful way, he used to be 10, 11, and 12
my son might have played on my lawn,
might have walked on the sidewalks,
in sunlight, just maybe, it would have been lighter, sweeter.

A Bumper Sticker

"You had me at neuro-plasticity,"
I laugh, and so do you.
Aphasia, silence, tongue-tied, muffled,
let me explain with my notes: one second, let me see it, there, yes,
    I got it.

Sometimes, I can think of the world,
and I can be thinking, flowing, moving, dancing in a field,
    progressive tense.
Now, yes, I can imagine it, yes, it is—was—beautiful.
I can dream, I can elect, I have power, yes, I can do this, watch me!

Global, Broca, Mixed non-fluent, Wernicke, Fluent, Anomic,
    Primary Progressive, Aphasia.
There are two million others learning to speak again, and, yes,
Neuro-plasticity, you had me hopeful, speechless:
I hope.

In Good Company

I wonder about Dan Gilbert being struck
completely incapacitated
I wonder how his stroke felt.

I wonder how Teddy Bruschi was struck
two times—oh, my—once,
struggled, improved,
played football, announcer, ESPN and then, BAM!
I wonder how that would feel twice.

I wonder about Miles Davis, who played a plaintive trumpet
wondering if he could do this.
My, what a piteous, yet melancholy song
Kind of Blue
Birth of the Cool
Porgy and Bess
Sketches of Spain
Bitches Brew
Miles Davis, 1926, 1991, stroke.

I wonder about Winslow Homer—
Left and right
Breezing up
The gulf stream
Undertow
The life line
Snap the whip

And Kirby Puckett—
the 1991 World Series Hall of Fame
and I smiled with Kirby's win

I wonder at
marvelous, heroic Walt Whitman.
He wrote dozens and dozens
Leaves of Grass, 52 poems, yes!
The Open Road
Song of Myself
O Captain! My Captain!
And he had a severe massive stroke

I wonder about Isabella Stewart Gardner,
a collector,
Woodrow Wilson, Richard Nixon
two presidents,
such prominent people
all struck by stroke

I wonder about them all
breathing, working, struggling, improving
I listen, and I wonder what will happen.

The Black Swan

A small, slight, slender swan paddles the pond.
Ever so slightly, a swan gracefully glides, smoothly, gently, peacefully,
    as quietly, rhythmically he flows.
Look at it: how nimbly, lithely, it flows.
How I envy him.

But, below the graceful tips of glide,
the swan is churning, pulling, frantically, desperately even, making
    the legs work, ever churn, ever pull, ever frantic, works hard, real
    hard, for each stroke.

Aphasia.

Someday, one day, I, too, will speak it.

Sisyphus

With tremendous self-aggrandizing,
and craftiness and deceitfulness,
 Zeus, equally sullen, demanded, irked.

That a king, once Sisyphus, a king with guile,
killed guests, palaces, yes, travelers.
Zeus, angered, disappointed, and vexed
to displeasure Sisyphus, naked, cold
forced his pushing the stone, upwards, up the hill.
Zeus, what retroject, this conniving him,
Cackle, elephantine, iron-fisted Zeus?

Push, bump, prod, pull: the smooth and heavy stone,
Exhausted, crawl to an echoing sound.

Aphasia, I can push, but, silently,
I tug, like Sisyphus, quietly—Heave!

Meditation

I think, I know, at least for eight seconds, I know,
STOP:
Stop, listen, the practice, present moment.
Take a breath, four seconds, hold it, breathe.
Observe, look around you, attend to what you see.
Proceed, open your eyes, slowly,
breathe, four seconds, hold it, now, release,
and begin anew, the world that it is.

Ms. Malaprop

Malaprop, only seven words,
Or is that eight words, instead?
Malaprop, how many syllables?
I mean, she's as strong as an allegory,
Or, rainy weather can be rather hard sciences, or is it sinuses,
     or an alligator?

Ms. Malaprop gets it.
Officer Dogberry says, "Our watch, sir, have indeed comprehended
     two auspicious,"
or is it: apprehended two? too? suspicious?

It is easy to laugh at Ms. Malaprop, or aphasia, when a
     mispronunciation seems funny.
It's hard now, Aphasia, it comes from mysterious ways.

I have no delusions, or allusions of the past, or flying saucers,
     or just optical conclusions.

I'm no doctor, but I'm losing my patience.

Aphasia, I can get it, but sometimes, I sink.
Just remember, patience is a virtue.

If Only I Can Speak

A gray, dreary day, and he is excited,
"Mom, mom, I got in, I'm going to Scotland!"

It is here, he is accepted, but I quietly can only listen: "I'm accepted!"
I can think about him, 20 years old, and all I can feel is sadness.
I can hear him, but, I cannot talk, yes, speechless.

For years, I could fluently speak, and then, golly,
we cycled to the Ferris wheel,
we cycled to New Bedford, 38 miles,
we cycled on the bicycle path,
we cycled for ice cream,
we cycled for Martha's Vineyard,
we flew to Arizona, and climbed that hill—hot, but we made it.
We flew for the Dominican Republican,
But now, he will adventure, but I am silent.

He turns away, walking, closed in his headphones,
thinking, pondering, musing, he walks away, and I can only say,
"congratulations, son; I am so proud,"
maybe.

Spring

On an any day, sun-shining mine eyes,
I can see this beautiful, wonderful scene,
and I imagine it, loving it, sparkling.

The sun rises, the spring fills me,
and, yes, it is pleasant, resplendent.
And wistfully on this day,
I can feel this ominous, foreboding,
because only with winter, is there spring.

Calliope

In speaking words, beautifully voiced,
Calliope presides over eloquence.
In a word, the epic poetry,
she sings, she rises, pellucid,
shares ecstatic harmony of her voice.

With Orchidaceous, she smiles, winsomely
or, like a goddess, dryad,
playing a muse, sonorous, resonant.

Clio, Euterpe, Thalia, Melpomene,
Terpsichore, Erato, Polymnia, Ourania,
in a chorus of muses, Calliope reigns.

One Thing

My closest, nearest, the most intimate
thing occurs, in all my life, the ischemic hit.
It happens, Saturday, 21 May.
I can't reach my breath: please, just one moment,
from twirling, swirling, whirling, just one breath.

I rush with the medic, from bedroom floor to chair,
arms outstretched, needing my phone.
They just don't know, they just don't know,
but, my friends, my God, how I love them,
Carolyn, my wife, Jackson, my son,
Chris, Caty, Father Robert, Betsy, Sandy, they know me,
    they understand me—
perhaps, they love me,
hold, hold, hold me, rise up,
hold me, gingerly, carefully.

37 days, Spaulding Rehabilitation,
My friends loved me, now Alison, now Chris,
Now LaRoy, now John, now Karin, now Denise.
Now, crippled and taking small steps,
I can smile, it's good, my arms can still hug.

What is the one good thing that has come from my injury?
You, all of you.

One Other Thing

In a world with everything,
I can do only three things:
be kind, be kind, be kind.

Haiku

I have aphasia
garbled with words, I'll make it—
confusing, helpless

A life, full of love
advocate, connect, listen
only life, above

Communication
disorder not intellect
aphasia mantra

Rowing with strong arms
I'm feeling great, but I'm slow
one day, I'll be fast.

Present Moment

A soft, quiet feeling, shhhhh.
Relax, and feel the peace in my mind.
Focused mind, gentle ideas, slow the racing.
Calmly, the ideas flow, as the heavy burden floats by.

Five minutes, ten minutes, twenty minutes, I can feel it lift,
the weight, leaving my shoulders light.
Sensations, yes, therapeutic and easy.

Relax: it is an awareness of the present moment.

A Thanksgiving

Juniper and birch, aroma whelms,
the dulcet cranberries roam our room,
stirring them, sugar, pecans, raisins.
The peeler unravels the red potatoes,
slices the white bits and cores the orange.

The smooth dormant chicken tenderly
washed away with blue, surgical gloves.
Meticulously the abolition.
With a stir, the butter rises up,
and the stuffing can rest, only five minutes.
With orange peel, rosemary, thyme, pepper,
I brush the olive oil, and the salt,
cramming away, waiting.

The sweet potatoes and the mashed ones,
Bubbling, perking, filling up
as the cranberries and collard greens await.
Pepper, salt, olive oil, all the routine,
onions, red flake peppers, mayhap with cranberries,
    or bergamot of a seville tree,
or cedar, or oranges;
a theme, really, I can use more pepper.
I finish the rice with coconut milk.
I plump the blueberries in the corn bread, and I wait until it is ready.

A feast really, a fulsome, pantophagous feast,
Awakened with a prayer and dinner.

With My Beautiful Daughter, Liza

With my own, I'll sing with a smiling stance.
I'll sing with laughter, you can laugh, too.
My friend, I can smile and laugh with you.
Sometimes, others frown or glance, or make weepy sounds,
lachrymosely, sounds of illness,
or disdain, or lamentations, sullenness, contempt.
Oh, yes, how hard, or how disconsolate
to listen to lies or prevarication
to hear noise, or evil, immorality.
It is dark, dank, and feeds inside ourselves.
In your company, I am freed from it all.
From the mirror, a younger, stronger self will rise up,
and in you, my friend, my daughter, I can see
the happiness that envelopes my life.

Compline

On dark clouds, shadowing the night,
I keep the silver lining, when it's you.
A night prayer, prayers each night, thinking and praying for you.

Lord, forgive me, please, let me be.
Lord, I have sinned, let it rest.
Lord, I have trespassed on us, let it lie.

"Completorium," thank you for every easy day.
Bless us lord, forgive me, Lord,
And when entering the dark ways,
Remember that sign of silver lining,
Of completion of the working day.

Hello

I am just dumb, it's just too hard for me,
I am stupid, I'm stuttered, and I cannot go on.
Aphasia, yes, but everything is too much.

I fumble, I work, it's too much,
I am heavy, I'm frustrated, angry, tired, fatigued, depressed,
    please help me.
But, with the Lord, I can at least pray.

And on one day, I will understand
both you and me—
have patience.

Farrago

In my mind, many different types,
severities of Aphasia with myriad names:

Global aphasia, reaching out for words.
Most severe, recognizing few words and no spoken language-
words locked away.

Broca's aphasia is severely reduced,
that haunting voice with short utterances.
UGH—I can hear it now, halting with effortful quality of speech.

Wernicke's aphasia, almost fluent, effortlessly fluent,
but with reading and writing severely impaired—
why can't you hear me, why so far from normal?

There are a variety of others,
Anomic Aphasia, Primary Progressive Aphasia,
    Mixed Non-Fluent Aphasia,
all aphyllous, keeping me in this cold, dead winter.
But, yes, I struggle along with aphasia, needing to express myself:
can I say something, can I express it?

I know what I am; I am what I speak.
I can hear it, listening to my words,
hoping my words will make sense of myself.

Empathy

I listen, I hear you, and I understand
I can hear you,
with kindness and with compassion,
I hear you.
I understand.
I listen.

Sign Language

With a massive ischemic stroke
I lay for 37 days, listening,
and I had one thing, aphasia.
I could turn around, mix up, stumble,
but, I just could not face reality.

Every day, I spoke my little signs,
and yes, I haltering said and fumbled,
can I please have tomorrow?
Practice, practice, practice, and, yet,
I can't speak it, okay, well, then, all right.

But, what if I could use sign language?
Yes, you know, for the persons *sans* words?
Sign language, now that is beautiful.
I could say, "I forget," with a palm sweating away, oh, that is splendid.
I could read hand signs,
Speaking fluently, eloquently, persuasively, laughing, and smiling.
Hand signs, seemingly singing a song, quietly,
    expressing the world that is.

In a small gesture, I cross my heart: you.

Speak the Speech

In a word, I am vexed,
I am irritated.
Aggravation, anger,
flustered, discontentment,
seething, humiliated
bitterness, resentment
annoyance, vexation,
anxious, disheartened.

Yes, these are the words
when I'm telephoning
feckless, I can hear myself.

Aphasia.
Can you hear me?

The Light

The light, the truth, I am.
The truth, I am the light,
I am the truth and I am the light.
Confusing, isn't it? Aphasia blocks the light,
but these are confusing and uncertain times,
unaware and anxious, broken and uncertain,
but words still comfort,
I am the truth, and yes, I am the light.

In This House, I Believe

In beauty and in kindness,
Black lives matter, oh, yes, always:
Keep eyes on the prize.
In sunset, in life, in belief, in faith.
In life science, yes, real science,
the Big Bang, evolution,
oh, yes, God has His hand, omniscient.

In real love, love, together, clasped hands.
No humans are illegal; a person has a right to a trial, no slavery,
    no trafficking;
and, yes, in our home, we believe in kindness, beauty, curiosity, laugh-
    ter, and love,
a soulful life.
We believe in life: that is real.

Alexa

Each day, when I arise, I remind myself what day it is, and what time it is.
Knowing the day and time
I can feel safe, feel home, feel comforted.
With aphasia, this is the work I do.
Alexa, what day is it, what time is it, and tell me a joke.
It is someday, anytime, and where do pencils come from?
Pencil-vania.

Daniel, Feet of Clay

Majesty, look you, awesome appearance,
The head of the statue was made of pure gold,
its chest and arms, silver,
its belly and thighs, oh my, bronze,
its legs of iron, its feet of iron
and partly baked clay.

Yes, it is majestic, ready to arm.
I'm ready for battle, I'll win them all.

Funny: an ischemic stroke shattered me,
A weak, small, tender clot left me without words

With all my thoughts, I can barely speak
I'll stand anew, I'll speak with aphasia.

A Maelstrom

Suddenly, the blackout shuts out light.
No sound, no color, nothing's out.
I'm frightened by the black sound.
No feeling in my bed, no lamp, no light.
No desk, no carpeting, nothing, all black.

I am standing, feeling, tentatively, the all-black sound,
    touching it, tenderly.
I'm anxious, worried—ouch, Damnit!
The winds cracking the branches outside.

Immediately, the light is out.
I can see the whiteness of the sheet,
And I'm contented, comforted, with its white:
I can feel it—a bed, a lamp, my desk, covering the light veneer
    of mine own
I can hear it, outage silence, no whirring sounds.

It's all right, maybe it is a few minutes, a few seconds.
Imagine, what it will be, when I can see it;
I'm all right with the sights and sounds.
For now, I can sit down and rest.

Lagniappe

Can you feel it, kept in one room,
37 days, imprisoned,
sheltered: look at my feeble hands,
Left hand, I can hardly lift it.

There I am, yes, fettered, locked up,
Spaulding Rehabilitation.
I can smell, flowers, rose, sapid,
I can feel tulips, lilacs,
Just waiting to be out there, pausing.

Then they freed me, immured me, released me.
The sun opened mine eyes, and I was free.
My wife unlatched the door: I opened,
And I saw the bursting sun—
it was June, and I pressed on the car window,
Dunkin'—it was free—Starbucks—it was free—Chipotle—oh, my,
    it was free—
and everything was free, there beyond mine arms.

Freedom, 37 days, liberty, might I say, emancipation—
    did Juneteenth happen?
No matter, I was free, and I was alive,
The safe, beautiful, clean, warm, safe world
Ready to spring—is it almost summer, yes!—
and begin anew, stepping tentatively, with my weakened left arm
    and hopeful speech.

At Rest, At Peace

With so many swirling
angered minds,
violent persons,
COVID-19, I rest now, uneasy,
a bit dis-eased.

I am anxious, I am worried, I am tense;
With my anger,
I lash out, saying something,
with fisticuffs I imagine:
blow, blow, I hit them with words,
thinking I'm speaking, but nothing comes out.
I am exhausted, I am tired, I am troubled.

But, I will be okay:
with love, with compassion, with empathy,
I will be all right.
Listen first, connect second,
And love, always.
I cannot fight with you:
No, I will listen, I will connect, I will love.
We will each take a tremulous step,
and with faith, we will get there,
gently, holding our hands.

About the Author

Michael Obel-Omia is a public speaker, writer, and educator who has aphasia due to a stroke in 2016. In his tireless efforts to improve, he has found poetry allows him to express himself in ways that speech cannot. An avid advocate for people with aphasia, Michael has published essays about his experiences in the journal *Blood and Thunder: Musings on the Art of Medicine*; *The Boston Globe*; *The Providence Journal*; and Rhode Island's NPR *This I Believe*. Michael lives with his family in the beautiful town of Barrington, Rhode Island.

CPSIA information can be obtained
at www.ICGtesting.com
Printed in the USA
LVHW022050120423
744168LV00003B/679